SUPER SCIENCE TOOLS

USING A THERMOMETER

By Abigail B. Roberts

Gareth Stevens
PUBLISHING

Please visit our website, www.garethstevens.com. For a free color catalog of all our high-quality books, call toll free 1-800-542-2595 or fax 1-877-542-2596.

Cataloging-in-Publication Data

Names: Roberts, Abigail B.
Title: Using a thermometer / Abigail B. Roberts.
Description: New York : Gareth Stevens Publishing, 2018. | Series: Super science tools | Includes index.
Identifiers: ISBN 9781482464092 (pbk.) | ISBN 9781482464115 (library bound) | ISBN 9781482464108 (6 pack)
Subjects: LCSH: Thermometers–Juvenile literature.
Classification: LCC QC271.4 R478 2018 | DDC 536'.50287–dc23

Published in 2018 by
Gareth Stevens Publishing
111 East 14th Street, Suite 349
New York, NY 10003

Designer: Laura Bowen
Editor: Therese Shea

Photo credits: Cover, p. 1 Image Source/Getty Images; pp. 1–24 (series art) T.Sumaetho/Shutterstock.com; p. 5 (left) Westend61/Getty Images; p. 5 (right) 5 second Studio/Shutterstock.com; p. 7 PhIllStudio/Shutterstock.com; p. 9 (left) Tom Wang/Shutterstock.com; p. 9 (right) OlegDoroshin/Shutterstock.com; p. 13 Tim Boyle/Getty Images News/Getty Images; p. 15 (top) MaeManee/Shutterstock.com; p. 15 (bottom) Kameel4u/Shutterstock.com; p. 17 Arthur Palmer/Shutterstock.com; p. 19 (left) Don Bartletti/Los Angeles Times/Getty Images; p. 19 (right) Andrei Kuzmik/Shutterstock.com; p. 21 (right) rawf8/Shutterstock.com; p. 21 (left) iofoto/Shutterstock.com.

CPSIA compliance information: Batch #CS17GS: For further information contact Gareth Stevens, New York, New York at 1-800-542-2595.

CONTENTS

Boldface words appear in the glossary.

How Hot?

Let's make candy! If you heat the candy mix to a certain **temperature**, it'll be soft when cool. If you heat it to a higher temperature, it'll become hard. Thermometers are important tools that measure temperature. We need them for candy—and science!

5

Up and Down

You might check a thermometer to find out the temperature outdoors. It helps you know if it's hot or cold outside. The thermometer shown on page 7 is a liquid-in-glass thermometer. It uses a special liquid that changes with temperature.

As temperatures rise, the liquid in a thermometer warms up. The liquid's **molecules** spread apart and take up more space. That's why the liquid rises in the tube. When the temperature falls, the molecules move closer. The liquid falls in the tube.

hot

cold

9

Reading a Thermometer

Thermometers that measure air temperature may show two kinds of **units**: Celsius and Fahrenheit. People in the United States often use Fahrenheit (F), but most other countries use Celsius (C) units. See how the measurements compare on page 11.

	°F	°C
boiling point of water	212°F	100°C
normal body temperature	98.6°F	37°C
room temperature	68°F	20°C
freezing point of water	32°F	0°C

11

When you read the temperature on a liquid-in-glass thermometer, the thermometer should be upright. Your eyes should be even with the top of the liquid. The number next to the liquid's highest point is the temperature.

Thermometers in Science

Doctors use thermometers. Some thermometers measure body temperature in the mouth, while others measure it in the ear! The temperature reading can tell us if we're ill. Sometimes, the thermometers are **digital** so they're easier to read.

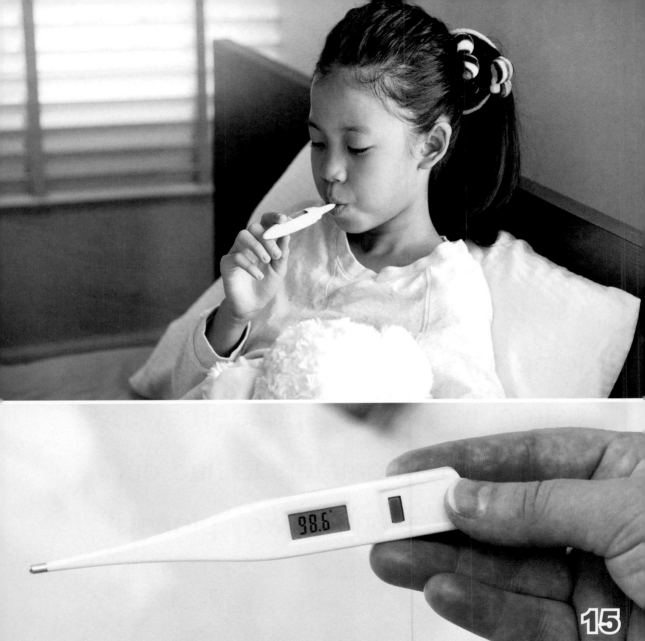

Some thermometers help us figure out temperatures from far away. **Infrared** thermometers use **lenses** to measure surface temperature. Scientists called astronomers study space. They use infrared thermometers to find out temperatures on faraway planets!

45.4℃

11:52   ε:0.95

OK

17

Special thermometers are needed in science for very hot and very cold temperatures. They might not look much like thermometers! Resistance thermometers use **electricity** to measure temperature. They're very exact and measure temperatures more than 1500°F (816°C)!

resistance
thermometer

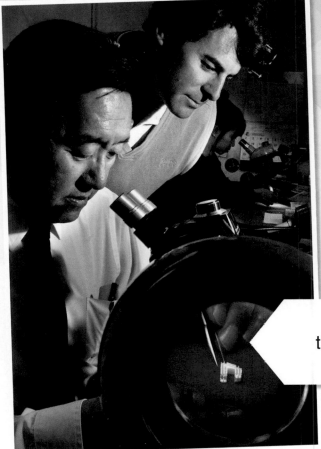

resistance
thermometer for
space shuttle

19

Scientists are making new kinds of thermometers. One kind is so small you can't even see it. It can measure the temperature inside a **cell**! It might be used to fight illnesses someday. Why do you use thermometers?

You Use Thermometers!

1) Use a thermometer to measure the inside and outside air temperatures.

2) Write them down.

3) Circle the higher temperature.

GLOSSARY

cell: the smallest basic part of a living thing

digital: showing numbers rather than using a pointer or marker that must be read

electricity: a form of energy that is carried through wires and is used to operate machines

infrared: producing or using rays of light that people cannot see and that are longer than rays that make red light

lens: a clear, curved piece of glass or plastic that changes the direction of light rays

molecule: a very small piece of matter

temperature: how hot or cold something is

unit: an amount of length, weight, or temperature that is used for measuring

BOOKS

Gardner, Robert. *How Hot Is Hot? Science Projects with Temperature*. Berkeley Heights, NJ: Enslow Elementary, 2015.

Hughes, Susan. *Is It Hot or Cold?* New York, NY: Crabtree Publishing, 2012.

Metz, Lorijo. *Using Thermometers*. New York, NY: PowerKids Press, 2013.

WEBSITES

How Thermometers Work
home.howstuffworks.com/therm.htm
Read more about the inner workings of thermometers.

Make a Thermometer
www.energyquest.ca.gov/projects/thermometer.html
Ask an adult to help you make this thermometer.

Thermometer
nationalgeographic.org/encyclopedia/thermometer/
Find out about more kinds of thermometers here.

INDEX